FUEL

A 40-Day Devotional

Kevin Duel Raines

 www.trafford.com

North America & international
toll-free: 1 888 232 4444 (USA & Canada)
fax: 812 355 4082

A special THANK YOU to the sponsors that

contributed toward the publishing of this book.

Betty Raines - In Memory of Luther Raines

Ronnie Raines

Ken & Sherrie Kagey- In Memory of

Quinard Shelnutt

Gracie Sutherland

Anna Maddox

Hunter Clark

Rusty & Cheryl Clark

Sue Lasseter

Sandy Brown- In Memory of Robert Kagey

The Jones Family

Melinda Abreo - Realm Rest Ministry

Joyce Ortiz

Lucretia Gonthier - The Lighthouse PCH

Joyce Burnette

Christina Taylor

Promises Do Come True!

Dedicated In Memory of Mildred Maxwell

INTRODUCTION

I have searched for an "it" in many things, looked for "it" in people and other religions. To discover a relationship with God through Jesus is more than a religion. A relationship with Jesus is more than a fix. Some may say, "There is too much dying in Christianity, too much judging, too many *don'ts*."

I apologize for those who misrepresented the message of Christ in that way. I have discovered through several attempts of suicide and many types of addictions that I really wasn't living. I wasn't truly walking out my destiny. A relationship with Jesus has been the best decision in my entire existence. *He* has given me a new opportunity to be the real "me." I know what it's like to wrestle with identity, to seek every day vigorously, wanting to know true purpose. Hey, what a discovery I have found!

I encourage you to just start a conversation with God today. He will surely respond. The secret to hearing the Creator is you must silence the other voices getting to you. In the silence and stillness is where you will find *Him*. It's *Jesus*!

When you look at the reality of it all . . . I'm just a messed-up, sexually assaulted country-town kid and high-school dropout who almost succeeded in taking his life twice. *But to God*, it's about the promised word that was spoken at the time of my creation. It's about an adoptive bloodline that *He* designed me to be strategically grafted into, that overrides any stigma that man might have labeled me as. It allows me to have a "new birth" and a "new start." It's truly not what people say about you but what God said about you before creation. The question is, can you hear what He is saying about you?

The enemy is trying to miscommunicate what has already been spoken about your existence over who you are. That's why Jesus spoke the words: *the truth shall make you free*. The truth to your existence and the truth of who you are created to be is the *real* you.

Then said Jesus to those Jews which believed on him, If ye continue in my word, then are ye my disciples indeed; And ye shall know the truth, and the truth shall make you free.

—John 8:31–32 KJV

My prayer is that this devotional will encourage, challenge, and prompt you to ask more questions about God and who HE is to you and in you.

—Kevin Raines

DAY 1

THE MOUNTAIN

Name something you tolerate to live with daily.

Name something you couldn't live without.

To change conditions, you might have to change positions.

With a steep mountain, there are three facts that cannot be mistaken.

1. You ascend, change location in elevation.
2. Your body position changes the further you go.
3. Not everyone will or can make it to the top.

There are two examples of mountains that are handled in two distinctive ways. One type of mountain is that which Jesus said we could speak to, and by faith, it would be removed. The other, by example, is the mountain we must journey to discover a deeper understanding for the climb.

The mountain could be said that it is discriminating; it creates that kind of offense in people against those who can't climb to the top. The mountain remains open for all who would like to give it a try. You can't discriminate against something that only provides an opportunity. You (the climber) decides if you fail or succeed. Don't blame the mountain.

Stop blaming the Mountain Maker. The mountain is simply an opportunity for you to make a discovery of yourself. Your mountain cannot define you. Your mountain will set you up for an opportunity to define and discover who you are and what you are made of. The mountain is not partial but practical. What you see is what you get. You cannot discuss the issue with the mountain, but the mountain will create the conversation on how you must change yourself to get over it. It's not what is inside the mountain that brings the conflict and frustration but the condition inside yourself toward climbing it.

And after six days Jesus taketh Peter, James, and John his brother, and bringeth them up into a high mountain apart.

—Matthew 17:1 KJV

Some places we go with Jesus will require more than just a yes but a commitment to pursue.

NOTES

NOTES

DAY 2

THE HOST AND THE WORSHIPPER

I'm so intrigued by the incident with the women washing Jesus's feet and the Pharisee host, Simon (Luke 7:35– 47).

The Pharisee invited Jesus into his home yet questioned His capability of being a prophet. He only talked "about" Jesus. When people invite Jesus into their hearts yet still question His purpose and capability, they speak from only a mouth movement.

A woman comes in Simon's home, stands at the feet of Jesus, and then goes beyond the chatter of talking "about" Jesus. Her desperation was greater than the conversation.

We have got to move beyond the talk of who Jesus is and get past the fears of what others are calling us. It's time to become real worshippers.

Her worship spoke louder than the conversation in the room. Some people talk about loving Jesus, while you can easily see that Jesus talks about those who show Him their true love, a full-motion love that moves the heart of Him. I want my worship to go beyond talk notion and become full motion.

You did not give me a kiss, but this woman, from the time I entered, has not stopped kissing my feet. You did not put oil on my head, but she has poured perfume on my feet. Therefore, I tell you, her many sins have been forgiven—as her great love has shown. But whoever has been forgiven little loves little.

—Luke 7:45–47 NIV

NOTES

NOTES

DAY 3
Past Out

Moments from our past, whether failures or successes, can be used to create a character who will be beneficial for our present. Whether it is learning to work through the setbacks, recovering from a fallout, or learning to work it out despite the controversial circumstances, you will be able to pull from the past. There are qualities that you will develop by getting through your past. What could have destroyed me will now be used to promote me.

Your enemy will pull from the pain of the past to try and destroy your present. Parts of your past are nothing but promotional pushes that drives you into purpose.

Don't you dare get weary in well-doing. What the devil meant to destroy you with, God will use to promote you. What the devil meant for evil, God will work for your good. David learned from his past battles. He learned in defeating the lion and the bear, among the sheep, out in the fields of purpose, and in how to move when confronting the giant. His past battles prepared him for the ultimate purpose. If you are going to reflect on the past, let God reveal to you the promoting potential elements you gained from it. Don't let the enemy assist in repaving a road for you to return there and dwell. Your battles are for a reason, in season, or because of a decision.

And David said unto Saul, thy servant kept his father's sheep, and there came a lion, and a bear, and took a lamb out of the flock: And I went out after him, and smote him, and delivered it out of his mouth: and when he arose against me, I caught him by his beard, and smote him, and slew him. Thy servant slew both the lion and the bear: and this uncircumcised Philistine shall be as one of them, seeing he hath defied the armies of the living God. David said moreover, The Lord that delivered me out of the paw of the lion, and out of the paw of the bear, he will deliver me out of the hand of this Philistine. And Saul said unto David, Go, and the Lord be with thee.

—1 Samuel 17:34–37 KJV

NOTES

NOTES

DAY 4

CONVICTION TO BUILD

What has happened to true conviction? Have we continued daily with such perplexed ideology that we have forced real conviction out? Jesus spoke a truth in the Gospel of Matthew, how the last days will be likened to the days of Noah. The ark was a place of kingdom preservation, a sacred place to continue God's kingdom. The ark was built out of obedience, not out of success or comfort to man. The ark was not built to show what man could do but rather what God would do. Only eight individuals continued with a sincere conviction to build and responded in daily surrender to the conviction to build something bigger than themselves. Mankind lost the will to build something beyond themselves, to protect and preserve something beyond mankind.

Could there have been more arks? I believe there could have been more arks. How, Kevin?

The instructions were given to a man with a conviction to see God's kingdom prosper and for God's will to be accomplished. The instructions were given with one requirement— *build*. There was only one set of instructions needed for them to build. The instructions would not have required more plans only for more of man to follow through with the plan.

The instructions have been given in the Holy Word of God for these last days. We stand likened to the days of Noah. It's your choice whether you build or not. Whom will you let stop you from building? What will you allow to distract you from building? What will you allow to silence your conviction to build?

Build. There's a kingdom coming.

But as the days of Noah were, so shall also the coming of the Son of man be. For as in the days that were before the flood they were eating and drinking, marrying and giving in marriage, until the day that Noah entered into the ark.

—Matthew 24:37–38 KJV

NOTES

NOTES

DAY 5

YOUR CHOICE

So many times, we have in our mind that it's God we are waiting on. Too many moments slip by while praying the same old prayers. We sit idle and do nothing but wallow in "pity thinking" that we are yet "super spiritual" because we are waiting for God to do something. We have become lazy, complacent, idle, and comfortable in that position. So many times in scripture, we see the word *choose*. God has provided. God has made a way. God has given answers. God has given above and beyond to mankind everything he needs to succeed. It's time you do something. *Choose what to do.* Make the choice to pursue. Make a choice to step out. Make a choice to go beyond. Choose this day whom you will truly serve. Stop acting like God's child, and start choosing to be God's child.

And if it seem evil unto you to serve the Lord, choose you this day whom ye will serve; whether the gods which your fathers served that were on the other side of the flood, or the gods of the Amorites, in whose land ye dwell: but as for me and my house, we will serve the Lord.

—*Joshua 24:15 KJV*

I call heaven and earth to record this day against you, that I have set before you life and death, blessing and cursing: therefore choose life, that both thou and thy seed may live.

—*Deuteronomy 30:19 KJV*

KEVIN DUEL RAINES

NOTES

NOTES

DAY 6

PUT THE LID ON IT!

It was near lunchtime, and I had started cooking a new type of grain. I was following the instructions pretty close. The instructions had advised to put the lid on it and let simmer for the remaining twenty minutes after bringing it to a boil. I started peeking inside the cooking pot after the first five minutes of simmering. When I peeked the first time, it didn't seem to be too big of a deal, noticing no change. After numerous attempts of peeking under the lid, my expectation was growing increasingly negative. I'm down to the final five minutes on the timer and still *no change.*

I thought to myself, *This will have to be thrown out . . . this stuff is no good. It hasn't changed. Maybe it sat on the shelf too long. Maybe it just didn't do what it was supposed to do, or maybe it was just me and my cooking skills.* Then an interrupting thought came to my mind: *put the lid on it.* There are still five minutes to go.

I put the lid back on and waited. I looked at the timer and still pondered the main question: how is it going to change that fast? If it hasn't done what I thought it was supposed to do in the amount of time given, how do you really think five minutes is going to make the difference?

After five minutes, the timer went off. When I lifted the lid and looked, something had *shifted*. Something had *changed*. Within minutes, the consistency and texture had changed. It had *increased*.

You may be in a place where you have tried and tried to follow the instructions (God's Word). You may feel you have sat too long on the shelf. You may have considered that it's just not working for you. You may be ready to throw everything out. *Put the lid back on it*. Time might be crunched, and you may not have seen change the first five times you looked, but keep watching and waiting. Keep your faith up because I promise you, God is moving in the things you cannot yet see. The timer hasn't sounded yet; even in the last moments, *God* can make what seems to be impossible possible, and *you* will see a change. *Put the lid on it!*

Then Jesus said to her, "Woman, you have great faith! Your request is granted." And her daughter was healed at that moment.

—Matthew 15:28 NIV

"For my thoughts are not your thoughts, neither are your ways my ways," declares the LORD. "As the heavens are higher than the earth, so are my ways higher than your ways and my thoughts than your thoughts."

—Isaiah 55:8–9 NIV

Trust in the LORD with all your heart and lean not on your own understanding; in all your ways submit to him, and he will make your paths straight.

—Proverbs 3:5–6 NIV

NOTES

NOTES

DAY 7

FORGIVENESS

Those who are feeling the guilt and shame of past sins, let me remind you that it has been forgotten. It is in a sea of forgetfulness. It has traveled from God's mind as far away as the east is from the west (beyond comprehension). God's grace is sufficient.

In many cases, it's our guilt of trying to live in perfection than live through the promise of God. We have been embedded with the performance of perfection from parents, friends, coworkers, and even ourselves. We have experienced the repercussion of man's reaction to our failures, but God is much different. It's a good thing to feel God's conviction and then to repent of sins in our lives, but it's not God who brings the feeling of shame or guilt. That feeling is manifested from the power of our flesh and the power of darkness. If that stays within us, it can lead to doubt in God. Know that when you confess your sins before God, you are forgiven the moment you ask.

God's greatest disappointment is not in our attempted failures or falls. God's greatest disappointment comes from when we no longer showcase the need for His existence in our daily lives. We simply try and do it on our own without Him.

Conviction is man's inner voice that speaks, acknowledging the truth. There is a Creator in existence above himself.

No conviction is the evidence of one's inner voice that turns from the knowledge and truth of the Creator's existence.

What parts of your life has God become extinct in?

And he said unto me, My grace is sufficient for thee: for my strength is made perfect in weakness. Most gladly, therefore, will I rather glory in my infirmities, that the power of Christ may rest upon me.

—2 Corinthians 12:9 KJV

He will turn again, he will have compassion upon us; he will subdue our iniquities, and thou wilt cast all their sins into the depths of the sea.

—Micah 7:19 KJV

As far as the east is from the west, so far hath he removed our transgressions from us.

—Psalms 103:12 KJV

NOTES

NOTES

DAY 8
THE DOOR

~~~~~~~~~~~~~~~~~~~~~~~~

I stand at the door and knock!

<div align="right">

—Revelation 3:20

</div>

"I am the door," Jesus said.

<div align="right">

—John 10:7

</div>

The word for *door* used here is *thyra* (thoo-rah), defined as "opportunity, an entrance, a way."

Open to a teacher—one who encourages hope—for the most successful results.

Christ is seeking entrance into souls and those who comply with His humble request. Salvation is not about your access to heaven; it's about Christ's access to you. Salvation is not accessing the door to a heavenly paradise but Christ accessing the door of your heart. It's not about a place for where we are going but the places in our heart we allow Christ to move. This exposes the fact that anyone can live a certain way and not feel guilty about entering the house of someone else. But when someone is invited to see how you live, it changes the conditions and the mental response to how you must live.

Salvation is not about you accessing someone else's door; it's about someone accessing your heart's door. It doesn't matter what you make or take in financially. If we gave what was truly requested to be a disciple, we would all be in a dependency on God, greater than what we are now. There is still so much "selfish motive" inside one to hold on to what God has said, "Let go of." It's not what your materialistic possessions and man-given titles are that move Jesus; it's what you are willing to give up.

Stop judging godly success from the content that's in men's wallets.

NOTES

NOTES

DAY 9

SPIRITUAL MOUNTAIN-MOVING EXPERIENCE

I want to see God move in places money can't buy.

I want to see God move beyond the areas of "humanistic" breakthroughs.

We say we pray and trust God and yet immediately pop a pill to ease the pain. We say we have faith to believe in the unseen but then undermine our prayers by finding every way to make it be seen. When we attempt and don't receive, with our time restraints, we use the term "God must not want it for me." Like . . . what?

I'm ready to see mountains move!

Spiritual mountains can represent the hurt that was created within your family before your time. Mountains can represent the curse that has loomed over you since birth. Mountains can represent a major blockade that has always been a distraction in your path. You have chosen to always go around it. "Speak to it,"

Jesus said. Jesus, You don't understand. Speaking to it would defy the requirements for a "miracle of man." You reply, "You know, Jesus, that would require a real unexplained miracle— something to happen that would have to go beyond human capabilities. A kind of faith that would uproot every explanation, the kind of faith that can't be described except for using the words *had to be God.*"

I'm tired of staying around things we call "miracles" that are still justified by man. I want to see something that goes beyond things justified in the natural. I'm ready to experience the supernatural in ways, such as dead men walking again, blinded eyes seeing, lame men walking, mental illness completely wiped clean, and *people* really set *free.*

I want to experience the power of the Creator who set the ocean's boundaries, who told the sun to stay, who gave life as we see it today.

I want to encounter the *One* who can set a fire yet can't be consumed, *One* who can break a river's course to see millions get their breakthrough, *One* who can cause birds to bring bread to you like in a drive-through.

I'm tired of my worship being so man-made, I'm ready to worship the *One* who goes beyond the grave.

I'm past wanting to see trees moved by a sword; I'm ready to see mountain's move through my Lord.

For verily I say unto you, That whosoever shall say unto this mountain, Be thou removed, and be thou cast into the sea; and shall not doubt in his heart, but shall believe that those things which he saith shall come to pass; he shall have whatsoever he saith.

—Mark 11:23 KJV

NOTES

NOTES

DAY 10

PURPOSE!

Purpose may not always be practical. Purpose may not always be pretty. Purpose may sometimes be painful. Purpose will always reveal a promise. Purpose will promote. Purpose will expose provision. Purpose is powerful. Purpose is planned. Purpose needs to be passionately pursued.

You are never too young to start a purpose. You are never too old to stop a purpose. You are never too far to begin a purpose. You are never too close to embracing a purpose. You are never too weird to have a purpose. You are never too you to be without a purpose.

In whom also we have obtained an inheritance, being predestinated according to the purpose of him who worketh all things after the counsel of his own will.

—Ephesians 1:11 KJV

The most challenging goal in life is discovering purpose. When you acknowledge there is a Creator, a Higher Being, God Himself, you realize you don't just pick purpose; you discover it.

You were designed for a specific purpose. You were created for this moment, this life, and this time. Significant struggles in one's life can be revealed by learning to sometimes "walk away." Walk away from those things you may feel called for, and move in those things you have been purposed for. The key is sincerely communicating daily with the Creator. You were designed for a reason, for such a time; discovering that reason will be life's fulfilling joy.

Who hath saved us, and called us with a holy calling, not according to our works, but according to his own purpose and grace, which was given us in Christ Jesus before the world began.

—2 Timothy 1:9 KJV

NOTES

NOTES

DAY 11

BEYOND MY REFLECTION

Today we are obsessed with image. We have become enamored with "being ourselves." We are engrossed with the wrong image. Our prayers have become silent as our chants become wilder. "Mirror, mirror on the wall, who's the fairest of them all?" We don't have to worry about other idols becoming the center of religion because we can't keep our focus off ourselves long enough. If you stay in a land of wondering all the time, maybe like Alice, you need to get away from the "looking glass."

There is so much more we possess beyond this shell. With God, the real source of power lies from within. We all came from dirt. We will all return to dirt. The miracle of creation was what God blew into a man, not what He created man from. Start recognizing the time you put in yourself versus what you put in front of yourself today. My true life success and inner peace will ultimately be discovered beyond my reflection.

Casting down imaginations, and every high thing that exalted itself against the knowledge of God, and bringing into captivity every thought to the obedience of Christ.

—2 Corinthians 10:5 KJV

NOTES

NOTES

DAY 12

MY WORSHIP

When your worship turns traditional, your encounter will be unspiritual. Tradition cannot fuel expectation. Expectation is the force that fuels the Holy Spirit's fire.

My level of worship will determine my position of reception. My level of worship will determine the intensity of my perception.

My worship can create spiritual war zones. My worship can signal out an SOS. My worship can defend me when my words are impotent. The depth of your worship will expose the depth of the Spirit.

My worship isn't just a thing I do, but what I do, I will do in spirit and in truth. We practice with groups to perfect our precision of sound while never perfecting our praise. There will be a difference in the sound.

Perfecting your praise will go beyond the natural ear into the inner ear of the Spirit. Perfecting your praise will require your willingness to pass the precision of the sound into a realm of practiced praise. Can I get a sound check?

If you want to look at a real worshipper, look at David. He worshipped out of his robe. When you worship, it doesn't matter about the status you hold in an earthly position, but it's the condition of your heart. David was a man after God's heart. It's time to put down the robe.

God is a Spirit: and they that worship him must worship him in spirit and in truth.

—John 4:24 KJV

My worship reflects my ways. My ways are the result of my habits. My habits are a product of my choices. My choices are determined by my decisions. My decisions are created daily.

It's got to be more than a cute saying. It's got to go deeper than the tickle of my ears.

If praise is not present, the production of sinful behaviors and self-willed intentions become more prevalent.

My ways are a product of my worship.

My worship reflects my ways.

My worship wrestles fear.

My worship oversees my intentions.

My worship keeps guard over my motives.

My worship denies me the right to be lifted up.

My worship resists the temptation for self-gratification.

My worship brings about the real character of God.

My worship inspires my faith.

My worship is the fragrance of my atmosphere.

Wherefore the Lord said, Forasmuch as this people draw near me with their mouth, and with their lips do honour me, but have removed their heart far from me, and their fear toward me is taught by the precept of men.

—Isaiah 29:13 KJV

This people draweth nigh unto me with their mouth, and honoureth me with their lips; but their heart is far from me.

—Matthew 15:8 KJV

NOTES

NOTES

DAY 13

How Long Do I Forgive? Do I Forget Too?

Jesus saith unto him, I say not unto thee, Until seven times: but, Until seventy times seven.

—*Matthew 18:22 KJV*

The answer is not the sum of the equation Jesus spoke, but the answer lies in the equation.

When studying numeric values and numerical symbolism in the Word of God, there is great revelation and insight given.

The number *seventy* can relate to a generation.

The number *seven* represents *completeness, spiritual perfection.*

So you could say the message Jesus was giving about forgiveness is if it takes a whole generation, a whole lifetime, or until you are complete . . . keep *forgiving.*

Forgiveness is what gives you *access* to heaven.

But if ye forgive not men their trespasses, neither will your Father forgive your trespasses.

—Matthew 6:15 KJV

Remember, true forgiveness also *means* forgetting.

For I will be merciful to their unrighteousness, and their sins and their iniquities will I remember no more.

—Hebrews 8:12 KJV

As far as the east is from the west, so far hath he removed our transgressions from us.

—Psalms 103:12 KJV

NOTES

NOTES

DAY 14
CALM DOWN!

Life has moments that can cause your lungs to feel as if they were submerged ten thousand feet below water in the deepest sea, trying to breathe. The pressure of feeling like that every move you take creates an even more overwhelming discomfort. Your mind races using the greatest question starters, such as *why, who, what, when, how,* followed by another question: is it ever going to get better?

In breathtaking, life-crushing, exhausting, devastating life moments, we must learn to activate the *Word of God* in our lives. It seems we consult everyone first before turning to the *truth*. We get advice from every blogger, tweeter, or Google answer before turning to the *One* who has made *the* answer available.

We must turn to and lean on God's Word. It is truly a simple life-altering decision. Use the power of faith today to calm a moment of fear, to shift the hesitation of doubt, to decrease the level of anger, to resolve the tension of strife, and to fight the fit of rage. *God* is the greatest answer to any question today you might be trying to find. *He* is the greatest motivator for any type of encouragement. *He* is the greatest booster to any down day. Give it a *real* shot. You will not be disappointed. Promise!

Don't worry about anything but pray about everything. With thankful hearts offer up your prayers and requests to God. Then, because you belong to Christ Jesus, God will bless you with peace that no one can completely understand. And this peace will control the way you think and feel.

—Philippians 4:6–7 CEV

I give you peace, the kind of peace only I can give. It isn't like the peace this world can give. So don't be worried or afraid.

—John 14:27 CEV

NOTES

NOTES

DAY 15

THE VOICE OF NATURE

But Jesus answered, "If they keep quiet, these stones will start shouting."

—*Luke 19:40 CEV*

Can you hear it hustling through the trees, every branch, every leaf? Can you hear the ground from the soil? Can you sense the boulders shaking from the depths of her noise? There is a rumble deepening like the bass beats. Turn your ear to accompany the sound it's bringing forth; she is speaking as your silent voice.

Can you feel the pressing of her waves as she drowns the sounds you are to make? Can you hear the wood creatures with their song they are singing in your place? Our rhythm has turned to motionless idle, while her song is getting louder and louder.

We must not be deafened by these matters. Rise and take your place in this hymnal in courts of praise. Lift your voice from within to discover your shout desired by *Him*. If we choose to stay silent much longer, Mother Nature will replace our voice, and we will be beaten out of life's most impactful moments. Rise with angels among men. Sing out with a voice of triumph. Take your rightful place again!

May our cries be like fire purging the darkness, turning it brighter, singing with our voices once again. May our movements come with motion, creating a sound like thunder that spreads like rain in sanctions of wonder, and may our praise be louder than the others.

Your faith is the intro, your voice is the key, and your movement is the beat that brings the melody. Your heart sounds the first note, and your life is the song's theme, so make your life a song and sing.

NOTES

NOTES

DAY 16

A MODERN-DAY JUDAS

Judas walked right up to Jesus and said, "Teacher!" Then Judas kissed him.

—*Mark 14:45 CEV*

We have allowed the complacency of a Judas mentality to come in and sweep our hearts. We parade up and showcase our intimacy toward Christ in public places, when behind closed doors, our hearts have negotiated deals that gratify only ourselves. We have taken for granted the position Christ gave. We show off our public affections toward Christ among the ones we are attempting to impress. Our motive is hinged on making pennies on a dollar. We put more focus on how much we can make on the exchange for the revealing of Christ. Do you find yourself displaying your affection for Christ more in the presence of others than in your time alone? May we see the compromised state of Judas that lead to self-destruction. May we be aware and vigilant. May we not grow so complacent on our works that we forget the greater *One's* work at hand.

Food for thought: there were many types of people at the foot of the cross the day of the great sacrifice. Some sold and argued over the parts of Jesus. These were, by tradition, soldiers and defenders—the ones who actually carried out the crucifixion. They were trained to enforce "the law." There were others who stood in awe to discover the price of a true hero. He gave up His opinion to give an opportunity for others to have a chance at freedom. They were captivated as the words of pure love came out of His mouth.

The truth is every person that day was standing equally on the same leveled ground. Stop arguing over the pieces of Jesus. The garment he wore was useless when it came to the price of the sacrifice. Is your focus on the parts of Jesus or the price He paid? Are you trying to defend a piece of Him that is useless in another's liberty? Trust me, there is an audience watching to see just where your focus lies (John 19).

NOTES

NOTES

DAY 17
A New Look!

For many individuals, a scar can be the reminder of a great tragedy, a traumatic moment, or a life-threatening altercation. Scars can be visible many times through an outward display on the skin. Many times, scars are much deeper, applied to the heart or brain. Emotional scars can be the worst to endure. But today every time you look upon the scars, take *a new look*.

Let that scar not remind you of the pain that once was attached to it, but let it be a reminder, a sign that you are still here, and *you survived it*. Let it serve notice to the fear that it tries to bring upon you. Let it serve notice to the ill-willed emotions that rise from the inner glance you take to it. *You* are still here, and *you* overcame.

Rejoice that *God* is faithful to *heal* that which once was broken, torn, and wounded!

I *am* still here for a reason. I will not let my scars define me. They will develop me into the ultimate design of the Creator's ultimate plan for my life.

To appoint unto them that mourn in Zion, to give unto them beauty for ashes, the oil of joy for mourning, the garment of praise for the spirit of heaviness; that they might be called trees of righteousness, the planting of the Lord, that he might be glorified.

—Isaiah 61:3 KJV

NOTES

NOTES

DAY 18

THE CHANGE IN IDENTITY GREEN PASTURES: DRIED-UP RIVERS

We spend so much of our lives trying to find who we are. Our identity is so important in the discovery of our purpose. Identity was the main subject of conversation between the woman and the serpent in the beginning, which still exists today.

While driving by a place where a significant amount of green grass was growing, my eyes became tightly fixed to its beauty. It "looked" so serene. It "looked" so peaceful. What seemed so beautiful turned very disturbing quite quickly. I realized that the beautiful grass was supposed to be a roaring river. I became saddened to think that even though the grass was bright and beautiful . . . water was absent. This place was never intended to be a green pasture but a roaring river. The river had dried up.

It became something completely different from its original creation. It was supposed to be a life source of water, not a source of life depending on water. It was originally planned to provide life to all the inhabitants that surrounded it. Instead, its beauty drained it from the more abundant supply. What used to supply life now must take from it in desperation just to keep its beauty. It lost the connection from the higher source, and now all that's left is the shell of the enclosing parameters that once used to be full. So what's the difference, Kevin? If it remained "beautiful," why complain? What's the big deal?

Your God-given purpose will always define your difference; your place will always direct it. Pursuing both will bring completeness to your life as well as the ones destined to be part of it.

The pivoting moment in my life in uncovering real identity was the day someone spoke out these words: "You were destined. You were anointed. You were called. You were talented. You were positioned for greatness, but you became something else."

Help me, God, to be all who I was created to be! Help me, God, not to see the beauty something can bring in mere Expression but to see the vitality of my true created purpose and the will to pursue. May my desires be unto You, God. I play a part in the plan.

Whoever believes in me, as Scripture has said, rivers of living water will flow from within them.

—John 7:38 NIV

For I know the thoughts that I think toward you, saith the Lord, thoughts of peace, and not of evil, to give you an expected end.

—Jeremiah 29:11 KJV

NOTES

NOTES

DAY 19

RAINBOWS

Being spiritually lost is like being blind. We see with our natural sight but extremely limited from within. We see so many things used with a rainbow symbol, for example, color, freedom, love, expression, and hope. While understanding where the rainbow originated from and its creative purpose, one should gain truth of origin. The original use of the symbol was clearly used as a coming-out declaration. It was not only used as a coming-out declaration but also as a coming-through and coming-over symbol of hope, love, and compassion.

We scream to be original, be yourself, be who you were created to be; yet we hypocritically oppose that objective with the same truth when those point out the hypocrisy that lies beneath the mere image on the canvas of life. We use images that have already been branded, and yet we still want to call them original.

How can we scream "Be you" when the very symbol of the same declaration is representing a denied truth? It's sad to try and comprehend where some of us placed our truth. I have discovered on this side of the rainbow; color goes beyond what man can see, love is shown to its greatest capacity, freedom extends beyond boundaries, and hope is an everlasting anomaly. When you simplify it all, I have uncovered a truth spiritually as well as naturally.

The truth is blind people will never be able to enjoy the true beauty of the rainbow. To see this truth, I had to come out. I had to come outside of the walls I had restricted myself in. In discovering this truth, I didn't just come out of the closet—*I got out of that house.*

And the bow shall be in the cloud; and I will look upon it, that I may remember the everlasting covenant between God and every living creature of all flesh that is upon the earth. And God said unto Noah, This is the token of the covenant, which I have established between me and all flesh that is upon the earth.

—Genesis 9:16–17 KJV

NOTES

NOTES

DAY 20

THE TRANSITION

I wait for the Lord, my soul doth wait, and in his word do I hope. My soul waiteth for the Lord more than they that watch for the morning: I say, more than they that watch for the morning.

—Psalms 130:5–6 KJV

Wait on the Lord, and keep his way, and he shall exalt thee to inherit the land: when the wicked are cut off, thou shalt see it.

—Psalms 37:34 KJV

What do you do when you have taken the test but haven't heard the results?

What is conceived in between the finishing of the exam and the results of the exam?

What is determined between then and now?

What will you do while waiting?

What will you choose to do while you are waiting?

What do I do in the transition period?

The transition period is so vital to one's journey. This is the place that can cause one to grip courage and continue or give up because the wait is too great. This is the place some have sat for too long. This is a place that some have called life's home. Some never truly step into promise because they give up in the transition.

Be confident in knowing you will make it. Even if you feel you are nowhere, you are still somewhere, and even if you feel you are a nobody, the fact remains you are still somebody.

God, I am determined to be faithful in the transition.

NOTES

NOTES

DAY 21

GOD: THE FIRST FASHION DESIGNER

Then the LORD God called to Adam and said to him, "Where are you?" So he said, "I heard Your voice in the garden, and I was afraid because I was naked, and I hid myself."

—Genesis 3:9–10 NKJV

Also for Adam and his wife the LORD God made tunics of skin, and clothed them.

—Genesis 3:21 NKJV

In today's giant fashion frenzy, it's so easy to lose sight from where the original idea of clothing was created. The garment you have on right now was strategically designed by a person for a purpose. The first purpose obviously is to cover you or protect you from exposure. The second purpose could be to bring a sense of confidence that will allow you to freely communicate with others. God solved a communication problem by giving a garment gift. The garment was a symbol of forgiveness and restitution. It was a kind act bridging the gap between man's fall and *His* grace. *He* used a garment to quite the chaos. *He* used a garment to give man the confidence to communicate again. Every time you are getting dressed, be encouraged that there is still hope. Through all my failures and attempts to hide from *Him*, one look at my garments will remind me that *He* still wants to communicate with me. *Never give up!* We have been given a "garment of grace"!

Food for thought: When you want to reveal yourself and remove your clothing or limit your clothing, it could represent a state of denial from *His* grace. It could be a symbol to subconsciously reject the garment He has given. Keep your garments on.

NOTES

NOTES

DAY 22

THE "TO DO LIST"

I hear people say, "That's not of the devil. That's not a sin. That can't affect me." I am convinced that the enemy of your soul can use "no-name paper towels" to bring separation between us and God. *What?*

What do you mean, Kevin? We compare our lives to a sin list, "a list of dos and don'ts" that label sinners from saints. It's supposed to separate saved from unsaved individuals. We feel better about ourselves if we can somehow "stick" to the list.

We are missing the point altogether. Being a Christian is not about a list of dos and don'ts. Being a Christian is recognizing the need for Jesus in our lives and submitting wholeheartedly to Him. It's about communicating with the Creator of our life and soul. It's about having a real intimate journey with *Him*. How can people question if there is a God? The simple reason people question God's existence is that they have yet to hear *His* voice. God's voice is like fire. When fire has been present in an area, there's no way you can return the items that were consumed back to the exact state they used to be.

When a person is not completely in a relationship with God, Satan will use anything to keep a wedge between them and God. Have you ever watched *My Strange Addiction*?

It's time we get past our "list to living right" and start living to list God as top priority in our lives.

For it is by grace you have been saved, through faith—and this is not from yourselves, it is the gift of God— not by works, so that no one can boast.

—Ephesians 2:8–9 NIV

Be alert and of sober mind. Your enemy the devil prowls around like a roaring lion looking for someone to devour.

—1 Peter 5:8 NIV

KEVIN DUEL RAINES

NOTES

NOTES

DAY 23
WHAT CAN I DO NOW?

"I want to see God move more in my life. I need a situation to really change in my life. It has just been a couple of weeks of pure hardness, sadness, and frustration. I feel I can't continue."

These are phrases individuals say across the world every day. In many life-pivoting moments that involved hardships and difficult times, I'm reminded that when Jesus came on the scene in a situation, three things occurred.

First, Jesus identified the need or situation. God knows who and where you are. He knows the very number of strands of hair on your head. You may say, "I don't feel like it!" It doesn't change the truth that *He* does! He is not caught off guard by the things that are happening in our lives daily.

Second, Jesus always identified the level of faith in an individual. Scripture makes many references in the ministry of

Jesus and how he would identify the level of belief in a person. Tears do not move God; faith does.

Third, Jesus gave an instruction or command for the individual to activate that faith, or in some cases, He commended an individual for activating their faith. We have created a "get it now" lifestyle in our society. We place an order, and in moments, we receive. Have we adapted this same form to God? Do we think we can just pray and expect to receive it within minutes, hours, or days, and if we don't we get angry or become frustrated at God? When we pray for a situation, remember, in many cases, there is an action required. God reacts to our acts of faith.

I am believing with you for true healing, help, deliverance, and wholeness in your life today. I am also believing that while you wait, you will be able to silence all the voices that are hindering you from hearing the voice of God. Listen to the instruction or direction that can activate your faith in the One who brings the miracle. This is your day. I celebrate with you.

Then saith he to the man, Stretch forth thine hand. And he stretched it forth; and it was restored whole, like as the other.

—*Matthew 12:13 KJV*

But Jesus turned him about, and when he saw her, he said, Daughter, be of good comfort; thy faith hath made thee whole. And the woman was made whole from that hour.

—*Matthew 9:22 KJV*

And he said, Come. And when Peter was come down out of the ship, he walked on the water, to go to Jesus.

—*Matthew 14:29 KJV*

NOTES

NOTES

DAY 24

GET TO STEPPING

There's a reason some individuals will never *step* into the calling of God. Some will never choose to *step* out of their complacency of comfort into a place of promised purpose. Others are unwilling to confront the fears that hinder them from moving forward. "The fear" of what you will have to leave behind and "the fear" of what you may have to face and conquer keep you from moving forward.

I am believing today courage is going to be actively present in your life. You will encounter supernatural strength and power to take the next *step* into purpose and promise, in Jesus's name . . . Amen!

The steps of a good man are ordered by the Lord: and he delighteth in his way.

—Psalms 37:23 KJV

For God hath not given us the spirit of fear; but of power, and of love, and of a sound mind.

—2 Timothy 1:7 KJV

Nay, in all these things we are more than conquerors through him that loved us.

—Romans 8:37 KJV

For all the promises of God in him are yea, and in him Amen, unto the glory of God by us.

—2 Corinthians 1:20 KJV

NOTES

NOTES

DAY 25

THE "HOW"

We are too focused on the *what*.

People do *what* others do.

What did you do to get your breakthrough? Answers are
  "I said this prayer . . .,"
  "I gave this seed . . ."

What did you do to get to that level? Answer is
  "I fasted four times and then prayed this . . ."

We try to implement the *what*. But you still seem to be getting nowhere. Why didn't I see results like they have seen them? Why am I not experiencing it the way they are experiencing it? The answer could be because you have inquired and focused on the wrong question and, in return, received a wrong, misleading answer.

Your focus should transition to "*How* did you get there?" "*How* did that happened for you?" "*How* did you?" No more "*What* did you?" The *how* reaches a deeper commitment level of faith more than just the *what* does.

The *how* allows you to see the persistence during the pain.

The *how* allows access to intimate details where the "what" leaves them out.

The *what* can't take you to the place like a *how* can.

The *what* can't totally communicate to you like a *how* can.

"*What* did you put in that cake to get it to taste so good?" The information received from the answer can lead to a frustrated unlearned "wannabe" cake maker.

But "*How* did you get that cake to taste so good?" creates a window of opportunity for you to see beyond just *what* it took.

The *how* is the substance behind it. The *what* is just a list of ingredients that takes to start it. Take the time to listen to the *how* behind a successful breakthrough you might have been seeking for.

Take the time to see the *how* behind the successor you have been watching. Take the time to study the *how* behind the mentor you are sitting under. We need to stop asking *what* Jesus did and start asking *how* Jesus did it. You will find that the *what* He did was merely a reaction to *how* He did it. The *how* always involved a *who*. And the *who* was always for my Father's sake.

This same principle applies. When we try to figure out *what* people are doing, it can lead to loss, frustration, and a wrong conceived perception of that individual. It takes a deeper level of compassion, faith, and understanding to look beyond the *what* they are doing and ask *how*.

NOTES

NOTES

DAY 26

PARTING WATERS, GAINING MIRACLES

But lift up thy rod, and stretch out thine hand over the sea, and divide it: and the children of Israel shall go on dry ground through the midst of the sea.

—Exodus 14:16 KJV

You say, "Only God can part these waters." With your faith, you begin to believe, and then you start to see waves.

You might be staring down at what seems to be a massive undertaking—maybe a life-drowning situation, an "impossible to get over" feeling, or a moment of hopeless frustration. The cries of those around you add to the building pressure of the taunting past still chasing you. You could be in a life-threatening situation like the children of Israel. Moses dared to believe that his obedience to

God's instruction and command would pay off and that he would see a miracle.

Persistence in your prayers, faith, and words makes all the difference. You *will* see movement. You *will* experience change. He raised his rod and stretched out his hand. He used a rod (symbol of power), with obedience and an expression of worship (stretched out his hand). Put your praise on it. Obey, raise, and praise!

Your faith predicts your change today.

I want to live out not the testimony of yesterday but the testimony of today. We continue to spread a life of testimony from yesterday's pain, sin, and hurt. I want to live today's testimony through grace, freedom and spread God's miracles. Your anointing isn't what impresses God—your obedience through faith does. Your calling doesn't gain access to His glory—your response to His instruction does.

And Moses stretched out his hand over the sea, and the Lord caused the sea to go back by a strong east wind all that night, and made the sea dry land, and the waters were divided. And the children of Israel went into the midst of the sea upon the dry ground: and the waters were a wall unto them on their right hand, and on their left.

—Exodus 14:21–22 KJV

You are waiting for your miracle, but what if your miracle is really waiting for you? The trick of the enemy is for us to spend a lifetime, trying to discover "what" we are . . . God destined in time a *life* for us to discover who we are. You will never discover what you are until you decide who you are. There's power in your testimony.

NOTES

NOTES

DAY 27

PROCESS

My access to Jesus is my daily process to freedom. Your behavior reflects your freedom you received through Jesus. The question is *if* the Son has set you free. How do I know *if He* has? You must believe!

What do you behave like?

Whom do you talk like?

What do you live like?

Don't pass the process.

Stop processing your past.

If the Son therefore shall make you free, ye shall be free indeed.

—*John 8:36 KJV*

Sin is just a visual manifestation of your level of truth, trust, and understanding of God.

We are born into sin because at birth, we have no understanding of our existence or purpose.

Sin is continued because a relationship with God is not greatly pursued.

A relationship requires reading what He wrote to you (Bible).

Your level of weakness to a sin can be overpowered by the matchless power of *His* strength; the deal breaker to victory is your level of surrender.

Your persistence to resist your flesh provokes a greater presence of God.

And He said to me, "My grace is sufficient for you, for My strength is made perfect in weakness." Therefore, most gladly I will rather boast in my infirmities, that the power of Christ may rest upon me.

—2 Corinthians 12:9 NKJV

Then, when desire has conceived, it gives birth to sin; and sin, when it is full-grown, brings forth death.

—James 1:15 NKJV

Until you start practicing the Word, you will never perform with purpose.

NOTES

NOTES

DAY 28

THE CHAIN GANG

Unbelief is a chain, and a chain is a symbol of limitations. You can still move your mouth to say, "I *am* free," and yet still be so limited in your movement to reach a breakthrough. If you are saved, the power of the chain has been broken. The reason you haven't gotten free in your movement is because you are still holding on to the following limits you put on yourself:

1. Limits by how your day was

2. Limits of your current relationship

3. Limits of fear

4. Limits of false expectations on others

5. Limits of offense

6. Limits of hatred

7. Limits of religion

8. Limits of tradition

9. Limits *you* can drop if you just drop the chain

It will give you access to movement. It will bring freedom. We use our emotions and expressions more for everyone and everything else than the *One* who gave them to us.

Demons have more emotion and belief in Jesus than some Christians. We are more moved by the negative things of life than the positive things. Drop the chains!

NOTES

NOTES

DAY 29
NO MORE LABELS

Man has put labels on people for years, and labels never came from God. *Stop* throwing judgment at people. It's *not* your place. Labels define people to a category that was only created by the judgments of men.

Jesus came to save a lost world. Every one of us fits into the category of lost. If you have found Christ, your mission is to *love*. Throwing judgment on others is simply labeling one another to a category that is *not* your position. Our position is to *share* the *good news*, not to defend it (Romans 2, Matthew 7, John 8).

If we could spend more time preparing the way for the presence of God to move in our midst and less time trying to defend it, we would see more *change* in *all* of us. #NoMoreLabels #loveCovers (1 Peter 4:8).

I'm no longer defined by what I was but who I am. The real always upsets the fake.

NOTES

NOTES

DAY 30

SPIRITUAL CANNIBALISM

Now more than ever, we must be reminded to not get caught up, trying to compare ourselves to one another. The society we live in is a "dog-eat-dog world," they say. Matter of fact, news outlets recently have aired and posted studies on the real taboo and why we call cannibalism weird. Really? We are struggling inwardly because we continuously compare ourselves to other's looks, achievements, behaviors, successes, accomplishments, lifestyle, etc. We are feeding so much on the nature and compulsion of man that we are already consuming ourselves.

Note to Christians: We are no longer to be pleasers of ourselves but of His righteousness. Repenting is turning from our ways and desires and submitting to God and the plan *He* has for us. We are too busy tuned to what's happening in the lives of *The Walking Dead*, and that is why we can't see the dead things walking in our lives. In those moments of weakness, remember first God is made strong.

And he said unto me, My grace is sufficient for thee: for my strength is made perfect in weakness. Most gladly therefore will I rather glory in my infirmities, that the power of Christ may rest upon me.

—2 Corinthians 12:9 KJV

But seek ye first the kingdom of God, and his righteousness, and all these things shall be added unto you.

—Matthew 6:33 KJV

NOTES

NOTES

DAY 31

PROVISION

The story of Abraham and Isaac going to the top of the mountain to worship speaks volumes because of the courage and faith it took to carry out an assignment that God requested. Sometimes we try and ignore the voice of God because we feel *He* might be requesting too much. I was drawn to the part about the ram provided at the top of the mountain. God provided for the two gentlemen at the top of the mountain.

When we pursue God with an *all-in* attitude, we will see the provision. While walking through some challenging moments, God reassured me through a simple revelation of this word. If I had provided the ram at the foot of the mountain, they would have missed *me* in the climb. Our attention seems to be the most attentive to God while walking up the mountains of life. Our steps do not seem quite as hastened. The lamb you are searching for may be on the other side of this climb. Don't forget to communicate while you are commuting up the mountain. Provision is awaiting.

And Isaac spake unto Abraham his father, and said, My father: and he said, Here am I, my son. And he said, Behold the fire and the wood: but where is the lamb for a burnt offering? And Abraham said, My son, God will provide himself a lamb for a burnt offering: so they went both of them together.

—Genesis 22:7–8 KJV

NOTES

NOTES

DAY 32

HEARING CONVERSATIONS

We have a choice on what comes out of our mouth as well as what goes into our ears. Communication is vital to existing on earth. Communication is also vital to existing in the afterlife, beyond this earth. Is your struggle to communicate becoming more and more apparent to you? Maybe it's the struggle to communicate with mankind, or maybe it's your struggle to communicate beyond human-life form, but you recognize there is a struggle with your communication. Your current communicable activity is crucial to your success or failure. Your discussions dictate your destiny.

Does your fight to thrive surpass your enemy's fight to kill?

Does your will to make a difference exceed your enemy's will to destroy your difference?

Do your conversations sound like the talk from heavenly realms or hellacious rants?

What you hear and what you listen to can be a life-changing expression. You may not always be able to stop what you hear, but you do have a choice to stop what you listen to.

Heaven and hell—both have conversations about you. What you choose to listen to determines which one becomes your truth. I refuse to let hell's conversation over my life become true prophesy.

Do not let any unwholesome talk come out of your mouths, but only what is helpful for building others up according to their needs, that it may benefit those who listen.

—Ephesians 4:29 NIV

Then he said: 'The God of our ancestors has chosen you to know his will and to see the Righteous One and to hear words from his mouth.

—Acts 22:14 NIV

NOTES

NOTES

DAY 33

DON'T SELL OUT IN THE MIDNIGHT HOURS

And the foolish said unto the wise, Give us of your oil; for our lamps are gone out. But the wise answered, saying, Not so; lest there be not enough for us and you: but go ye rather to them that sell, and buy for yourselves.

—Matthew 25:8–9 KJV

The light in you . . .

For God, who commanded the light to shine out of darkness, hath shined in our hearts, to give the light of the knowledge of the glory of God in the face of Jesus Christ.

—2 Corinthians 4:6 KJV

You must protect the gift inside of you that fuels you to shine (your oil). Don't allow the enemy to take from you that which causes you to shine. As darkness came, the presence or absence of oil became critical. Your oil can represent the preparation in preserving the light.

Do we make a priority in our lives to draw aside and make preparation to preserve the light? When the midnight hour comes we are prepared to shine. What looks like a hindrance today may be your help tomorrow. The value of their oil could not be purchased at that time. You can't put a price on this oil.

The foolish who didn't prepare for the midnight hour knew they would be seen only as wedding crashers. Without the light, they had sold out in the midnight hour and would only be viewed as just participating in a ritual, without thought of making it to the groom. Jesus Christ is the groom and is returning for us soon. They wanted to look the part to be among the saved but didn't make the extra preparation to keep the light burning in the darkest hour.

Don't sell out in the midnight hour.

Keep the "light" burning. *He* is coming!

NOTES

NOTES

DAY 34

THE BLESSING BUTTON

My grandpa had been given a barrel of buttons.

He was trying to clean out some things and came across the barrel and was debating on what to do with them. *Do I just toss them?* he pondered. As he sat there, God spoke to him to pray over the barrel of buttons and give them out to individuals as a point of contact, letting others know there is someone praying for them—a token of encouragement to the individual to let the receiver know it has been specially chosen and anointed just for them.

He had a choice in that moment to be obedient to such a bizarre instruction. He could have simply ignored the instruction and not be obedient. How crazy would he look . . . walking around, handing out buttons?

His one step of obedience set in motion the opportunity to reach out to countless lives. I became so inspired by the blessing button that I developed a bag line with buttons sewn on every bag, furthering the blessing button to others. It has and forever will impact my life.

My grandpa had a choice in that moment of decision. He could have let that "crazy instruction" become trash or treasure. He turned an issue into an opportunity. He turned a problem into a solution that went well beyond him. Obedience births impact.

Even when your mind can't wrap around the impact in the moment of its birth, God sees a far bigger picture. God is wanting those to take a dose of "crazy faith." He is looking for those who will step outside the box and be obedient.

My grandpa's act of obedience is what set purpose in motion.

Don't underestimate the significance of *one* instruction.

What do you have available that you have underestimated that God is ready to use?

The enemy is not scared of a physical change. He isn't scared for you to change your behavior. He is terrified of a person with a changed *mind*.

Obedience is better than sacrifice.

—1 Samuel 15:22

And this is love: that we walk in obedience to his commands. As you have heard from the beginning, his command is that you walk in love.

—2 John 1:6 NIV

DAY 35

THE BURNING BUSH ENCOUNTER

Moses, as we know him, had not yet parted the waters for Israel to walk on the dry ground. He had not gone before the great pharaoh and was still in a state of contentment after running from his past.

Moses was in the wilderness, content with his life. He had a family, a job, and was safely relocated from his past . . . until the burning bush encounter. God spoke one day through a blazing bush. He told him to take off his shoes. He told him *He* had called him to go back to Egypt.

Why would God call a perfectly successful, content man back to confront the place of his past? Why is God uprooting perfectly harmonious people up from their perfectly comfortable life?

Simple answer: *He has a plan.*

God's not calling you back to Egypt to rehearse your past failures. *He's* calling you back to Egypt to show your past failures what you have been rehearsing for.

God will never take you back to the place that smothered your fire, without first starting a greater blaze.

What tried to overtake you in the beginning will be overtaken by you in the end.

The first instruction at the burning bush was for Moses to take off his shoes. This signified that the place was a holy ground. His shoes being removed could also signify that his journey was about to change.

Encounter the fire of God today. Let His consuming fire purge you. Let it come in and bring direction. Let the fire consume you. He didn't ask Moses to get new shoes; He asked Moses to get a new view (Exodus 3).

NOTES

NOTES

DAY 36

KEYS OF THE KINGDOM

And I will give unto thee the keys of the kingdom of heaven: and whatsoever thou shalt bind on earth shall be bound in heaven: and whatsoever thou shalt loose on earth shall be loosed in heaven.

—Matthew 16:19 KJV

I have read this scripture so many times and heard it quoted for many years. I have always heard the phrase, "Jesus gave us keys *to* the kingdom." So many times, we glance at scripture and read over and over, word for word. While studying this very verse, I discovered there is a difference in the verse from what I'd studied in the past. The Word says, "Keys *of* the kingdom."

When I took a closer look at the two-letter word difference, I realized the vast difference it made. I was increasingly encouraged by the revelation. Giving access "to" something and access "of" something has different components. When we quote "to" the kingdom, we are retaining the information that would imply we have the capability to go to a place, to be a part of that place. When you have access "of" a place, it reveals the keys you possess grant you ownership or stewardship, not just accessibility.

Have we, as Christians, limited ourselves by the changing of a two-letter word? Many of us understand that we have access to the kingdom, and that is great, but we never take by faith the things from the kingdom that we need for our today. We only access ourselves *to* a thing and never fully understand we have access *of* it.

For example, someone who has access *to* our meeting place on Tuesdays has access *to* the building. I have been given the keys *of* this space; therefore, I have been given access *of* the whole building and not just *to* it. Jesus said, "I give you the keys *of* the kingdom," not just *to* it.

This revelation really opened my eyes. Jesus was stating *He* not only gives us the keys *to* heaven but also gives us the keys *of* the kingdom—free access to use all the resources there, not just access to heaven. It really confirms the next few lines of scripture and gives more of a powerful representation that whatsoever you bind on earth will be bound in heaven. Whatsoever you lose on earth will be lost in heaven. I haven't just been given the keys to the kingdom; I've been given the keys *of* the kingdom of heaven. Through Christ Jesus, you literally can have heaven on earth. You've been given the key. The Word of God will reveal the keys you need today for any and every situation, circumstance, or issue you may have or be going through this very hour.

Use your key.

NOTES

NOTES

DAY 37

DERAILED BUT STILL DESTINED

While visiting a church, a youth pastor was showing us the future home of their youth sanctuary. It was a massive facility that appeared to be under renovation. You could tell that something great had once been there but had been left abandoned or lost. She told us God had spoken to her to come back and help complete a vision that had been started years prior. Churches had come in and out but with every attempt, no prevail.

"A word from God was spoken over this property. This property is to be used for *His* glory." She added, "I've come back to help see it come to pass."

Immediately, my spirit man spoke inside of me and said, "Derailed but still destined."

You might feel in moments of your life that the "plan of God" has been derailed. You might feel that the vision or dreams God birthed inside of you have taken a derailing. You might be experiencing havoc in that family you thought was "God-purposed," but it seems to be everything but that. You realize, in almost a panic state, life has been derailed. Something seems to be lost, misplaced, taken a turn for the worst, left abandoned. And the question is . . . *What do I do now?*

The youth pastor kept sharing from her heart with sincere passion. God spoke again to my spirit man and said, "Watch what I can bring into your life that can restart the vision. Watch whom I can put in the path of your derailing who can be the support you need. Watch what I can do with what has been abandoned. Watch what I can do right in the midst of your derailing."

You might be experiencing a derailing moment in your life, but it—by *no means*—has canceled the assignment "destined" by God. You might be derailed, but you are still destined.

With God all things are possible.

—Matthew 19:26 KJV

Being confident of this very thing, that he which hath begun a good work in you will perform it until the day of Jesus Christ.

—Philippians 1:6 KJV

NOTES

NOTES

DAY 38

NO MORE LION AROUND

A caged circus lion might have been born into the confinement of man's law or cages, but he wasn't created to perform that way. He was created to take the throne of the lands given to him in the savanna to drive out the enemy and to protect all that was given to him within that space. It's not what you are born into; it's what you choose to accept as truth divinely designed by the Creator. I'm glad that through Jesus, we can be born again. In this day and time, second chances are what is needed to change our world. Truth is not what you feel to be true, but the truth is every word spoken by God. Let the lion lose. It's time for no more lion around.

God's grace is sufficient. If *He* shares it with you, then you find someone today to share it with too.

And he said unto me, my grace is sufficient for thee: for my strength is made perfect in weakness. Most gladly therefore will I rather glory in my infirmities, that the power of Christ may rest upon me.

—2 Corinthians 12:9 KJV

Jesus answered and said unto him, Verily, verily, I say unto thee, Except a man be born again, he cannot see the kingdom of God.

—John 3:3 KJV

NOTES

NOTES

DAY 39

LETTERS OF LOVE

The sun was rising, even though it could hardly be seen through all the rain. Goose bumps remained on the young girl's skin as she anxiously waited by the door. In spite of the chilly breeze forcing itself under the door, she continued to stand with great dedication and watch with great expectation. Her friend watches from the couch while curled up tightly in a blanket. The young girl eagerly watching by the door hears a voice suddenly say, "Maybe it's not today."

The young girl standing by the door softly whispers to herself, "What if it is?"

The girl on the couch added with slightly more force, "Why can't you just watch from over here, away from the chill that's coming from the door and window?"

The girl at the door breaks her focus for a moment to address what she believed to be a hideous question. "If you had read the letters of love that were written by him, you wouldn't be able to sit on that sofa so content."

The Living Word of God (Holy Bible) is "letters of love." If you never really read them, how can you expect to really know Him?

There is a significant difference in those standing at the door versus those on the couch; having a clearer vision to see the outside world is one advantage point.

Many struggle with where and how to read the "letters of love."

The "letters of love," when perceived not only with the mind but also in the heart, causes the reader to become a believer who mends a bond not easily torn apart.

Find "the letters of love" written in red (words of Jesus) and start there. Be encouraged and receive a revived spirit of dedication in spite of your current condition. Hold tight to the "letters of love."

But you are our letter, and you are in our hearts for everyone to read and understand. You are like a letter written by Christ and delivered by us. But you are not written with pen and ink or on tablets made of stone. You are written in our hearts by the Spirit of the living God.

—2 Corinthians 3:2–3

NOTES

NOTES

DAY 40

I WANT TO SEE GOD MOVE

Deciding factors to see God move

1. My perception of who God is

2. My measure of belief or unbelief

3. The amount of my participation

Stop waiting on God. *He* is waiting on us. Our involvement is crucial.

Why do I feel I am having trouble hearing from God? Often it's because there are too many voices fighting for the opportunity to be heard. First and foremost, we need to silence other voices, including our own. So we can be hearers of His Word. Faith comes by hearing.

God is what you believe *Him* to be. He is a savior through Jesus Christ. *He* is a friend, *He* is a healer, *He* is one who brings peace, and *He* is a provider. Jesus is my miracle.

If you only believe you have God to be a "Christian" just to get to heaven, then you will miss out on life here. You are created for a purpose. You are not saved just to go to heaven, but you are saved into the kingdom of God, on earth as it is in heaven.

Restlessness inside is usually a manifested sign of one who is on the verge of a breakdown. It's vital to communicate with the Creator.

Satan is the creator of breakdowns.

God is the Creator of breakthroughs.

What is being created in you?

NOTES

NOTES

Printed in the United States
By Bookmasters